Divorce Papers:
A Slow Burn

poems

by

Leslieann Hobayan

Finishing Line Press
Georgetown, Kentucky

Divorce Papers:
A Slow Burn

poems

Copyright © 2023 by Leslieann Hobayan
ISBN 979-8-88838-112-0 First Edition
All rights reserved under International and Pan-American Copyright Conventions. No part of this book may be reproduced in any manner whatsoever without written permission from the publisher, except in the case of brief quotations embodied in critical articles and reviews.

Publisher: Leah Huete de Maines
Editor: Christen Kincaid
Cover Art: Leslieann Hobayan
Author Photo: Leslieann Hobayan
Cover Design: Elizabeth Maines McCleavy

Order online: www.finishinglinepress.com
also available on amazon.com

Author inquiries and mail orders:
Finishing Line Press
PO Box 1626
Georgetown, Kentucky 40324
USA

Table of Contents

In Sickness 1

Un-love Letter 3

Listen 4

Ritual to Dissolve a Marriage 6

Reasons for Divorce 8

Trying to Uncouple Without the Kids Knowing Just Yet 10

Walking with Gabby 11

Thursday 13

The Waltz of Uncoupling 15

To Break Glass 17

Hinge 18

The Business of Divorce 19

Blue Mug 20

Sleepovers 22

Market Ready 24

Erase You from the Narrative 26

Be The Lighthouse 27

With Thanks 28

For my daughters

In Sickness

I knew it was over when I fell ill and you failed to care for me, opting to leave me alone in our bedroom, pain writhing in my bones like barbed wire. Did you know suffering multiplies in isolation like a zygote's cells dividing into more pain, exponentially growing until the suffering is insufferable and one is forced to break like a fever breaks like bones break like thresholds break and the isolation is so crushing that I willed myself into sleep to escape the pain (a hollowing out of bones from the inside out) to escape solitary confinement of the waking world—at least I had company in dreams, even if some were devils stabbing me with daggers in the heart— a nightmare from which I jolted, thinking I was dead—for certain dead— and felt relief, thinking I was released from pain, only to wake and find I was not. Only to find you asleep next to me, the gap between us wide as an ocean. It was already over. How I wanted to push you over the edge of the ocean-bed, to push you out of the room, to make you continue to leave me alone because it was better to be alone than face your failure in holding vows in sickness. You didn't know what to do with so much suffering, so you looked away, hoping my body would mend itself, hoping others would heal me with their deliveries of ginger tea and pho and essential oils. Even our kids knew what do to: instinctively bringing up bowls of soup of ramen of lavender tea, asking how I was, holding my hand, kissing my forehead. Their tenderness brought tears, relief. Theirs was a vast love, unconditional. What I did

to deserve them, I do not know. But you,
you faltered.
And I knew it was over.
I looked at the breaking, gathered the crumbling in my cupped hands and found myself
born anew

Un-love Letter

Dear Sir,

We regret to inform you that your appeal for more chances for repair has been declined. Unfortunately, you have submitted your paperwork past the deadline, and we can no longer accept it. Nevertheless, we read your request and would like to respond.

The plea for repairs to the connection of your heart to hers cannot be fulfilled. The problem does not lie in the idea of repair, for the link itself is not broken. It has simply expired. Like a carton of milk, soured in the fridge after some time. It happens this way sometimes. The passage of time slipping by unnoticed. And with that passage comes the curdling of milk. It is no one's fault. The refrigerator was cold enough. The other items—the zucchini, the shredded cheese, the raspberry jam—did not take away more cold than they needed. There was plenty of cold to go around.

In your case, sir, the link simply no longer works. You might try to jump start the electricity, but the wiring will not take. You might try to rewire the connection, but the ends are frayed. It has run its course and has since expired.

May we suggest a booster battery that can help you sustain your heart on your own until you are able to carry on independently?

Again, we apologize for these solutions that may not feel satisfactory, but this is the situation at hand. The options are very limited.

Should you have any questions or need further assistance, consult the owner's manual of your heart located in the corner that you have forgotten about.

We wish you all the best as you move forward.

Respectfully Yours,
Star Guides from The Order of The Universe

Listen

What do you want me to say? What do I need to
　　say in order for you to hear me, in order for you to listen

to really　　　unplugging your ears from the din of digital dings and sitting up and paying
　　　　listen

attention to what I am saying.　　Do you hear me?　　　Do you hear what I am saying?　　The sound coming
forth from my voicebox—the rounded edges of box tucked in the throat where my voice resides—the sound
pouring forth like a wave of ocean, of light, of frequency. What do you want me to say?
That I am done, that I want to move on? I have already done that even as my eyes
　　　　　　　　　　　　　　　　fall shut like heavy drapes

and I try to keep them open, but the fatigue is too great and the body is shifting into resistance: to turn
away—or is it something else? Is it self-protection? I can't discern one voice
from the next and what I really want to say I've already said.　　　Do I need to keep going to keep saying
repeating what it is I've already said, hoping that maybe one of these times the words will fall
on your tender eardrum, send the tiniest vibration through your body and maybe just maybe
finally you will get the message I've been trying to convey.

Or maybe not.

Perhaps I need to send the message in a bottle, through telegram, through Morse code, through telepathy, through dream. Perhaps then you will hear me, maybe you'll see me, watch my mouth form the shapes of words. Perhaps then you will finally accept
that it's over—

instead of trying to tiptoe closer to me, saying you'd watch that indie film with me, maybe try yoga—saying things that might get me to stay, as if I were a dog who stays when a treat is offered what do I need to say to get you to hear me?
to get you to
        let go—

Ritual to Dissolve a Marriage

Write your name in black ink
Write his name in blue
on white paper made from birch
the tree of new beginnings
Fold the sheet in half, top to bottom
Fold it again, right side to left
Fold and refold until the creases soften
Gently pull the paper apart
until four squares are made: your
names split
from one another
from each other
Gather these squares of paper
into a clear glass bowl
Gather the wedding bands
Gather a strand of hair
from him, from you
and place them in the bowl
Light a green candle
to open the heart chakra
Apply one drop of lavender
to your third eye, then rub
the rest on your palms, cup
them to your nose, inhale
Fill your lungs with forgiveness
with compassion
for him, for yourself
Light a cedar stick with the candle
chanting the spell over and over:
> *I release you*
> *I set you free*
bringing the flame to the bowl
igniting the paper squares
so delicate with ink
Watch each letter dissolve
in fire

And when the names turn to ash
and you taste it in your mouth
bury them with the rings
at the edge of the yard
where lawn and woods meet
There your marriage will rest
in peace and in love
There you say goodbye
then turn toward the sun
ready to begin again.

Reasons for Divorce

You make fun of my pants: white,
                loose, calf-length
    mimicking   fake karate moves
      an old familiar joke for these pants
        all in "good fun"
                      failing
  to see
      the subtle aggression—
You a white man: dealing
      a racialized joke
            to me, your Asian spouse
      and
    a non-compliment on my clothing choice
I can hear you now:
      this is not
           your intention
                and yet…

    there is a slip-out cop-out deal-out of responsibility
        "don't be so serious" you'll say
      if I point this out
                    dismissive

*

I say: because of our disconnect, our kids are full
                of friction, building—
    rubbing against each other like rough rocks
  hoping to spark a fire, set things ablaze
           and burn it down
No, you say, they're just being kids

            your gas lights my words to ash

*

I bite my tongue shrink my gestures
                tone down my clothing
                              hold back when you're near

When I speak up // you throw up a wall of stone // refuse

So I refuse this union // dispute its viability // break off, break free—

Trying to Uncouple Without the Kids Knowing Just Yet

It's a slow process. He is dragging his feet, refusing
everything. But you will not wait. You take action.

You started sleeping in a separate room a month ago,
hoping to get the message across: this marriage is over

Your previous attempts at conversation have fallen
on deaf ears and you are out of breath

But these things take time and you do not want
to upset the boat of your family just yet

So when your youngest cannot stop coughing
--her fits relentless—and she calls out to you—

When you attend to her and she asks if she can sleep
in your room, you agree and walk her down the hallway

and climb into bed with her in the middle of the mattress
because you do not want to answer any questions

about why you are not sleeping in your own bed. You want
only to comfort her, to assure her of love and safety

even at the cost of your own comfort. You sleep
like garbage, tossing, churning like a crumpled paper bag

in the wind, wonder if it's her coughing (should you go
to the 24-hr pharmacy for suppressant?) or the disconnect

between you and him that sucks on your energy
like a black hole, which only signals that yes,
                                    this marriage is done.

Walking with Gabby

"Do you think the American Revolution was a good or bad thing?"
"It depends on who you ask"

We take the familiar route down our street,
a slight downward slope towards the next block
then a left onto Fairfield.

She's holding the leash, our dog trotting
happily between us. The breeze still
has a chill and she is only wearing a sweatshirt:

charcoal cotton with a graphic heart over her actual heart.
I am snuggled in bright pink wool, fists stuffed
into pockets, purple scarf too thin

She yammers on, fulfilling her namesake, and suddenly
points out the man with his dog: "Stay away! Six feet! Six feet!"
she commands under her breath.

She is learning habits that go against our nature,
our desire to get close and I wonder how
this might play out for her generation.

She cracks jokes, tell me about her latest photo edit
of our dog, tells me she likes walking with me
because "Daddy doesn't like to talk about anything."

"When I ask a question, he says: go ask your mom."
and then proceeds to point out how much
he doesn't do around the house, how she sees

him on his phone or watching tv
while the rest of us clean up after dinner.
When she tells me this, we round the corner to our house.

She witnesses everything and I can't help but wonder
if she might choose a partner who will pull their own weight
Or will she do as I have and settle?

Thursday

Overcast windows
and there is that sameness
I want to rail against today
so I choose to redeem
my free birthday pastry
at Panera and message you
to add it to the lunch order
since I am in the midst
of teaching undergrads
about the art of performance
and crafting verse

Later, after class is over, I find
my cheese danish missing
from among the sandwiches and salads
(a small bit of the outside world in here)
and ask about it. You say
I never told you. I pull out
the message, point
to my words on a screen
and you say, impatient:
"I didn't read the whole thing."
as if it were my fault
you didn't read to the finish.

And here we are again:
you rendering me invisible,
not important enough to read
the message in its entirety
or is it your impatience, in general?

No matter.
You still don't get it.
Your failure to hear me,
to see me

for who I am—
And lest you think
it was a one-time thing:
the next day,
you completely forget
a word I said
about needing quiet
during my recordings
and run the vacuum's
loud open maw
to suck up dirt,
dust bunnies and hair
drowning out my words,
vanquishing them
to the pit of forgotten art beads,
stray Legos, lost bobby pins,
and dead marriages.

The Waltz of Uncoupling

Fifty-six days in quarantine
and we have found
a rhythm to our movements
navigating shared space
like a waltz
in which partners
                      do not touch

You move left   I move right
passing each other
in that narrow space between
the peninsula and fridge

Careful not to touch, there
are pauses in momentum
to let one pass
or redirection into another room—
a hyperawareness
that has become second-nature

I do not want to be near you
but we must stay put
in this same house
with our kids
who do not yet know
our plans to uncouple
because to venture out
in a pandemic poses risks
unseen, unknown

But what is life other than risk?
Each moment is not guaranteed
Each breath could be the last

So how do I imagine
a new life in this tentative existence?
How to imagine another dance
in which you live elsewhere
so I might salsa by myself
or merengue with our kids
to a wild rhythm
in so much open space
that I can spread my arms
wide across the kitchen
like a field of sunflowers
and the sparkle of a disco ball
											spinning

To Break Glass

to feel the heft
of melted sand
in your hands
clean, smooth, clear
cut edges—
to lift it up
above your head,
quiet mantra
chanted
under your breath
as you gather
the strength
and, standing
in the pit
of bike handlebars
old garden hoses
tattered roof shingles,
you slam down
the glass
listen to the satisfying
sound
of shatter & scatter
ricochet off steel
walls of the dumpster
and feel the break
of shackles
the slip
of weight
the jolt
of lightning

Hinge

We talk easily about the weather,
the latest number of new cases
of a virus that shifts its appearance,
re-openings and shutdowns—

The conversation flows
like an easy stream
gliding over rock and root

but always
in the back of my mind
the gears of divorce
turn slow
and I want to ask
if he's retained
an attorney yet
but restrain
myself, knowing
the delicate balance
required
of collaborative
unhinging:

a careful removal of the pin
from the knuckle of the hinge
so that each leaf each wing
might separate
and take flight

The Business of Divorce

What is your offer?

    amicable dissolution of marriage
    agreeable custody arrangement

What message do you have?
What transformation can you promise?

    red thread untying from our wrists
    loosening, as if gently pulled
    from a girl's ponytail, the hair
    falling undone, loosed to the wind,
    singing with the squeak of swing chains
                           back and forth
                 higher and higher
                                towards the sky
  Her laughter, an aria

What solution do you provide?

    an open meadow to spin freely
    arms open wide to swallow the sun
    and burst into the brilliance
                           you are,
    a brilliance that has lived
    within you all these years

Who are you?

    when you burn away all the layers
                                   you will know

Blue Mug

It slipped off the top shelf,
powder blue with white etching:
"Ocean City" with an image
I cannot recall now—
a scallop shell or an Adirondack chair—
    (memories of a long summer weekend
    when the kids were little:
    one chasing a balloon on the boardwalk
    laughter like wind chimes
    while the other two watched, chomping
    on fresh hot caramel popcorn)
                  —smashed to the ground.

You collected the pieces
made sure you had every last bit
and placed them inside the bottom half
                still intact

It sat on the counter for weeks,
heavy with your intent to repair
something that is beyond.

As the days went on, little by little
you painstakingly glued
each little shard back in place
until the mug was again made whole,
white fractures cracking
all over its blue surface

Now, it sits on the counter
next to the coffee maker,
waiting to be used—
but who would want to drink
from a broken mug?

                    What leaks might exist?
                    What flecks of glass float in the drink?

Today, I had the impulse to throw
it in the trash, this glaring metaphor
of our marriage— How you want
so desperately
to make me drink
from a mug full of glass
                      and call it love.

Sleepovers

Every weekend,
you have sleepovers
with your dad,
hopping in bed
where you think
I still sleep,
not knowing
I've been sleeping
on my studio couch
for a year and a half
as your dad and I
quietly untangle
the twenty some odd years
from each other.

The pretending
is slowly
killing me—
a burn in the chest
knotted at the base
of the sternum,
slight headaches
that linger too long,
sudden flared tempers
are a quick flash to release
the building pressure
of lies.

And every weekend,
I ask you, my youngest,
to whom I feel most
attached: when can
we have a sleepover?

Next weekend, you say.
I promise, you say.

But this routine
with your dad
has become habit
and you forget
what you said,
re-promising me,
already in his bed
every Friday night.

And one month goes by.
Then two.

And oh, how I miss my girl
wanting to nestle my nose
in your hair like I did
when you were a baby.
How I want to have you
curl your body into mine
before my time
with you is divided,
before you grow up
even more
than your eleven years
and sleepovers vanish
into thin air.

Market Ready

I try to straighten up the house.
Well, the counters really.
Okay. The peninsula.

There is too much clutter
that has grown and swelled
over these eleven months
of pandemic living
for me to even attempt
an appearance of neatness
before our realtor comes
to assess the market value
of this house we've lived in
for almost eleven years,
a house that has housed
our children as they have
grown from little girls skipping
in the wide expanse of yard
to the blooming young women
they are becoming,
the house that has held us
like cupped hands
letting us grow and thrash and
now finally separate—

Our realtor, an old friend and divorcé,
speaks frankly—piles of mail
on the counter behind him—
says we need to repaint the interior:
revere pewter, the color
of an overcast winter sky
right before the snow—

get the house in shape
to dazzle the buyer
so we can fetch a great price
and then divide our furniture
between townhouses.
Low maintenance, he says.
Great neighborhoods for the girls.

He sees your resistance—your grip
on the peninsula tightens—
tries to paint a pretty future.
He does his job well
as I lean forward in my chair
eager to move.

Erase You From the Narrative

Two years ago, I started removing
photos of you from my desk, sliding
magnets over your face on the fridge
that's covered in preschool art,
old permission slips, photo booth strips
of me and the girls from days
when we played hooky,
drove to the beach and skipped
on the boardwalk
in the late spring sun,
an April breeze too chilly for swimsuits—
played arcade games,
the blare of lights dazzling our eyes,
each game spitting out tickets
with every point scored on Skeeball,
the cranes a little tighter now
than during summer months
so we could each claw a stuffed animal
that we jammed in our coat pockets
which eventually got jammed in my purse
when we stopped for slices
at the spot where you could
get fries with that, the open sea air blowing
into our booth, seagulls gathering near
as we brought hot pizza to our mouths—

Before heading back home for ballet
and swim practice, we stop
at the water gun game and race each other
streams of water though the clown's mouth
as each seal rises up, up on its platform
bright red siren signals
that we all win
on this day without you.

Be The Lighthouse

What magic lives inside me—
the sparkle of earth fairies
working in the tunnels of my body
shifting muscle and fascia
loosening blocks, massaging stiffness
bones rearranging themselves
cell by cell
to redesign a new way
of holding the light
like a beacon

With Thanks

Words really cannot capture the depth of my gratitude for the people who have helped me in ways known and unknown through this difficult portal, but I will try (without making this page longer than the chapbook itself! Haha!). There have been so many beautiful souls who have walked with me to get to where I am now.

Deepest thanks to my teachers, both writing and spiritual, whose guidance has been invaluable all this time: Lee Upton and Mahan Rishi Singh Khalsa. Thank you both for your bright spirits and endless encouragement.

To my poet and writer friends who keep me going, who keep me putting pen to paper: Ross Gay, Veronica Corpuz, Emily Hyland, Rose Fitzpatrick, Claire Boyles, Lisa Factora-Borchers, The End Writers Collective, and the Community of Writers. Without all of you, this book would probably still be stuck inside my head. Thank you.

To my local friends who helped me keep it real: Mona Pan for all the Paris Baguette coffee talks to keep me sane while my world disassembled and reassembled itself; Pooja Makhijani for teaching me how to make bread and find comfort in the very act of kneading dough; Rosanne Zaltzman for sharing your own path which helped me navigate mine.

To my soul fam: Aly (Queeeen!), Tigre, Jess, Katherine, Joyce, Stacy, Holly, and Josh. Wow. What a trip it's been! What unfolding we are all experiencing! Thank you for being here with me.

To Lola Archer Pickett, whose expansive vision and sacred gifts have helped me see myself again, a self I had forgotten, a self I thought lost. Thank you for helping me return to me. I am infinitely grateful for our friendship and soul connection. Love you!!!

To my parents, Edgar and Mel, who have grown and evolved with me on this journey. Thank you for your love and support through this time. You don't know how much it has meant to me.

To my daughters, Marina, Gabby, and Sabrina whose radiant light and unconditional love fill my cup and inspire me day after day after day. Never stop being YOU (even if it irritates me sometimes. Haha!) Always celebrate who you are. I'll always be celebrating right there with you. I love you girls so freaking much!

Leslieann Hobayan is a poet, essayist, badass mama, healing artist, and host of the podcast, *Spiritual Grit*, a show at the intersection of spirituality and activism. She also has a weekly column on Medium called Maverick Mondays that share personal stories of racism, and Free Verse Fridays on Instagram, her weekly poems about healing and social justice. Nominated for a Pushcart Prize and a 2018 Best of the Net, her work has appeared in *The Rumpus, Aster(ix) Journal, The Grief Diaries, The Lantern Review, The Mom Egg Review, The World I Leave You: Asian American Poets on Faith and Spirit*, and elsewhere. She has been awarded the James Merrill Fellowship for Poetry at the Vermont Studio Center, a Mid-Atlantic Arts Foundation writing fellowship for a residency at Millay Colony for the Arts, and artist grants for Community of Writers and the Bread Loaf Orion Environmental Writers Conference. Currently teaching at Rutgers University, she's also the founder of Alchemical Alignment, a program for midlife women of color, teaches yoga & meditation, and facilitates sacred healing circles for people of color.

www.ingramcontent.com/pod-product-compliance
Lightning Source LLC
Chambersburg PA
CBHW022125090426
42743CB00008B/1013